RETROSPECTIVES

A COLLECTION OF AUTOBIOGRAPHICAL SHORT STORIES, ARTICLES, NOTES AND POEMS, BASED ON THE HAITIAN IMMIGRANT EXPERIENCE

———————

Maryse Noël Roumain

RETROSPECTIVES

MARYSE NOËL ROUMAIN
2007-2014

Edited by: Rachel Perry Kieffer

Retrospectives

To order additional copies of this book, contact Haiti Cultural Exchange at www.haiticulturalx.org. Telephone: 347-565-4429. Haiti Cultural Exchange is a non-profit organization.

Books by Maryse Noël Roumain are available at Haiti Cultural Exchange (haiticulturalx.org), a non-profit organization.

They include:

Evocations of My Past: Sketches of a Haitian Woman's Life

Evocations de mon Passé, 2

Haiti: Une Transition Bloquée

Anacaona: Ayiti's Taino Queen/La Reine Taino d'Ayiti

L'Enfant Haïtien et le Bilinguisme

Life Goes On, a Reflective Diary

Haiti Cultural Exchange Boutique

558 St. John's Place

Brooklyn, NY 11238

Tel: 347-565-4429

Table of Contents

Introduction

This is a series of texts written between 2007 and 2014. To these texts, I added two true stories and some poems conceived within the same time frame.

Those stories are not works of imagination but are related to my experience, my real life.

At a moment when the 2015 elections in Haiti reflect the weight of the Right and the Extreme Right in the voting process - through armed intervention, massive fraud; and the failures if not the complicity of the Electoral Board on the one hand and on the other, the divisions within the groups of the Centre and the Left, it is necessary to examine our political history to get to understand and propose.

Let us also keep in mind the next 2016 elections in the United States where there is a debate between the Social Democracy of Bernie Sanders, the Socialist candidate, and the Conservatism of the Right - Republican and Democrat.

This book will help to decide between these ideologies and policy options and the solutions that are presented.

Here are some texts that I have written some time ago to communicate with the world and with myself.

CHAPTER 1

A PRESENTATION OF BARACK OBAMA'S THE AUDACITY OF HOPE

(2006)

Obama, Barack. The Audacity of Hope: Thoughts on Reclaiming the American Dream. New York: Crown Publishers, 2006; 362 pp.

Barack Obama is best known for presenting and articulating novel ideas on the controversial issues that face us in this new millennium. His first book: The Audacity of Hope, Thoughts on Reclaiming the American Dream, proves this to be true.

In 362 pages of distinguished writing, the author scrutinizes the problems of America today and presents elements of solution grounded in a review of history and rooted in personal experience. What drives him is a strong and inherent desire to go beyond the polarization that still characterizes our times.

Obama proposes a synthesis of ideas based upon the belief as he says in his prologue that 'we have a stake in one another' and 'what binds us together is greater than what drives us apart.'

The author wants to go beyond the 'great political divide' that separates Republicans and Democrats and he opts for a bipartisan attitude and a political view that 'admits that the other side might sometimes have a point'. Conservatives and Liberals may be able to work together, he proposes, if they recognize that they 'all possess values that are worthy of respect.'

To support his view, he goes back to the founders of the nation and the Constitution of the United States which, he says, proved 'a defense against tyranny and all forms of absolute authority. Implicit in its structure was a rejection of the infallibility of any idea or ideology or theology or "ism", any tyrannical consistency that might lock future generations into a single unalterable course.'

Obama in this book criticizes the Constitution for not extending rights to the slaves and the Native Americans and he acknowledges that in U.S. history 'it has sometimes been the absolutists that have fought for a new order rather than the pragmatists, the voice of reason and the force of compromise.'

His ideas don't just cover politics. He also has thoughts on the economy, faith, race, as well as international relations and the family. On these questions as well, the author wants to unite rather than divide.

On the economy, he notices the emergence of a 'winner take-all' tendency which results for the working poor in a future of low-wage service work, with few benefits, the risk of financial ruin in the event of an illness and the inability to save for either retirement or a child's college education (p. 146). He criticizes the current administration's 'laissez-faire economics' devoted to tax cuts, reduced regulation and the privatization of government services and the belief that less government is a solution to our problems. And, he predicts as a consequence of this economic policy a greater economic and social stratification of American society exposed to the oil producers, underinvested in scientific research and workforce training, neglected of the environment, politically polarized and unstable.

To avert these negative outcomes, Obama proposes to build a new consensus that can make America more competitive in the global economy by investing in education, science and technology as well as energy independence.

Addressing the subject of faith, Obama presents himself as oecumenical and inclusive:

"Whatever we once were, we are no longer just a Christian nation. We are also a Jewish nation, a Muslim nation, a Buddhist nation, a Hindu nation, and a nation of non-believers."

Thus on this question too, he maintains a 'democratic discourse', resisting the temptation to impute bad faith to those who disagree.

On the subject of race, Obama, once again, promotes the respect of differences and the unity of the diverse races that constitute the American people: "There is not a black American and white American and Latino American and Asian American – there is the United States of America."

After the chapter on race comes the one on international relations or, as Obama puts it, 'the world beyond our borders' where he discusses and presents ideas about the policies the United States should entertain with the world. He goes back again to his experience having lived in Indonesia for a certain number of years (from the age of six):

"Indonesia provides a handy record of U.S. policy over the past fifty years... Our record is mixed. At times, American foreign policy has been farsighted, simultaneously serving our national interests, our ideals and the interests of other nations. At other times, American policies have been misguided, based on false assumptions that ignores the legitimated aspirations of other peoples, undermines our credibility and makes for a more dangerous world." (p. 280)

Obama goes on to plead for a coherent national security policy which the United States still doesn't have, he states, five years after September 11 and fifteen years after the breakup of the Soviet Union:

"We need a revised foreign policy framework that matches the boldness and scope of Truman's post-World War II policies – one that addresses both the challenges and the opportunities of a new millennium, one that guides our use of force and expresses our deepest ideals and commitments." (p. 303)

Finally, in addition to passages on the topics of immigration, healthcare, black ghetto life etc…Obama offers some ideas about policies on the family arguing against government interference in one's private life while presenting government intervention measures such as a child care policy that would alleviate the conflict between parenting and work.

So, what is The Audacity of Hope about?

Part biography, part history and part propositions, it is an appeal to conciliation and compromise, a successful attempt by the presidential hopeful to bring more coherence to our world.

CHAPTER 2

THE FIRE THAT BURNED MY SOUL

(2005 & 2011)

(1)

We are at the end of May. Soon it will be summer, bringing with it hot weather.

I have not been able to stand up or walk on my own, and have spent the past two weeks at my sister Marie's in Philadelphia. I am still shaken by what happened on Ash Avenue, where I live. I don't call to the incident by name to ward off bad luck.

I remember.

I am on the phone with my friend Ray who lives in Quebec, looking out my bedroom window. I watch thick black smoke rise up from nowhere to the 5th floor, my floor. From the window I see passersby on the street, their eyes directed somewhere below me. Their faces are fascinated and horrified, and I realize it must be a fire.

Not yet panicked, I pick up the phone and dial, 9-1-1:

-There is a fire in my building.

-What is your address?

-I live on Ash Avenue. There are firefighters here.

-Just a moment. We will inquire into what happened.

(A moment of fuzzy silence)

-We are sorry, but the fire broke on the second floor. There is no way to reach you. You have to wait until the fire is extinguished.

The panic comes all at once, all over my body. I scream into the phone:

-You have to do something! You can't let me burn alive!

I run back to the window, and crawl onto the fire escape. There are flames shooting out of 2B's windows, and the spectators yell for me not to try.

I'm back in the apartment. There is no way out through the entrance door either. A thick smoke has invaded the corridors.

I am thinking. I am thinking of the fire, of the progressive fire, of the flames and smoke climbing up to me. Victims come to my mind. Joan of Arc burned alive. She was burned in execution, for recovering her country from English domination, at only 19, tied to a cross, put on display and burned again. She's at the bottom of the Seine now, where fire can't touch her.

My mind jumps to lynching, neck lacing like in South African apartheid; like in Haiti, after the end of the Duvalier regime. I see a man wearing a tire around his neck; I see it lit on fire. I see him die.

I talk to God. I have a conversation with God. It seems to me my time of death has not yet arrived, not like this. I am working for Haiti, I am working for the world, I am working for God; and my work is not over.

Finally, the flames are gone from 2B's windows. I am not thinking straight, it seems. I take my sneakers off and climb back onto the fire escape. I race down the stairs, and when I reach the second level, that's when my feet burn. I descend the remaining stairs, running and screaming:

I am burned! I am burned!

The passersby look at me horrified. Some take photos.

(2)

At the hospital, the doctor finally comes in at 2:00 in the morning. He examines my bleeding feet. I ask his name. He answers, "My name is Liu. You've got a second degree burn. A skin transplant will not be necessary. The burns will heal by themselves after two weeks." Two days after, I was sent back home. From there, I left for my sister's in Philadelphia.

My husband is visiting from Haiti. He had planned to stay in New York with me and the kids, but joins me in Philadelphia. He spends his time walking around the pool, smoking and thinking. We take photographs of him, posing alone, serious. At dinner, he enjoys Marie's meals. She goes out of her way to be a generous hostess. He is served red snapper baked with onions, tomatoes and parsley and we drink good wine.

Later in the week, the two of us drive through the heart of the city. We pass the museum where Salvador Dali's exhibit has just ended. We eat oyster and scallop crepes at a Belgian restaurant, and for dessert, we share a sweet lemon crepe.

Not far from Marie's neighborhood, we see *The Interpreter* with Nicole Kidman and Sean Penn at a movie theater. It's a suspense film that takes place at the United Nations in New York, and Kidman is an interpreter who finds herself involved in a conspiracy to assassinate the African president of Motubo, an imaginary town on the black continent. African soldiers—mere children—fire machine guns at short range at the reporter who came to investigate the government's crimes. A bomb blows up a bus in Brooklyn; *The Interpreter, a must-see film.*

(3)

It was when I entered the apartment upon my return from the hospital that I was able to see the damage.

The firemen had forced the entrance door to see if there was anyone inside, and to verify the amount of smoke. Now, the door would not close. Was I to sleep in the apartment in such condition? My son and his girlfriend had scrubbed the blackened walls clean of soot, but the single bedroom smelled of bleach and smoke. I felt unsafe and scared. I had received no communication from the landlord about the cause of that fire. I worried about whether the problem was yet fixed.

I told myself the damage could have been worse: I did not lose all my belongings, or breathe fatal amounts of the toxic fumes like some of the other tenants. I noticed the two paintings my husband brought from Haiti on his last visit were spared: one is a Manès Descollines, three women bathing naked; the other is an abstract by Garibaldi, a lesser-known artist.

(4)

Three weeks after the fire, I write a letter to my sister Marie to thank her for having granted me hospitality.

As for my husband, he flew back to Port-au-Prince, to more political chaos than before his departure. I read on the Net that there are several dead and many wounded among the police and the civil population. The violence began to prevent the elections from happening at the end of the year. I try not to think what will happen if they do not take place. Our country does not need a complete occupation, especially since we are already significantly embarked on a path of dependence. The political parties are struggling to organize conferences, forming alliances, strengthening their bases across the country's ten departments. It seems there is finally a real willingness on their part to work toward a pluralistic society, political stability, and an economic program that will address the basic needs of the people.

(5)

I think about asking my nephew Jay to come to Ash Avenue and help me search for a new apartment on the Net.

Before the fire, I thought of decorating a little bit—colorful curtains in the living room, new tiles in the kitchen... I wanted to change the linoleum in the bathroom, to purchase a nicer bed frame. *Goodbye calf, cow, pig, couvée,* as the old fable tells. The fire burned my soul and fantasies. In any case, my salary at the library would not have allowed those extravagances.

I wonder if I can ever dance again to Gracia Delva or Coupé Cloué Haitian tunes. This morning I can at least listen to some good music. *Strings* plays through the speakers, then Cesaria Evora who is from African Cap Vert. Summer is not yet over, but later I will let Edy Brisseaux, one of my favorite musicians, interpret *Have Yourself a Merry Little Christmas* on his trumpet.

I tell myself I love the apartment, but not the building. I may as well look for another place nearby; someplace better, where I could have new dreams of redecorating, inviting over friends and family for dinners, dancing in the living room to Mamina's saxophone, or making paella.

(6)

Before he returned to the island, my husband and I sat in Tompkins Square Park, near my daughter's in the East Village, to breathe in the warm air. I must walk to tell my feet to work for me again. The park is filled with people.

"I wonder if the people who come to the park, are all from the neighborhood. They seem disconnected as if they do not have a rapport with one another," one of us said.

"Are they like us people of passage?" asked the other.

At the other end of the park, I recognized African drumming being played by some Puerto Ricans. On the way back to our daughter's, we stopped at a vegetable stand to purchase asparagus and red skin potatoes for dinner. At the wine merchant, we bought a bottle of red from South Africa. In the evening, I made myself a glass of iced chamomile tea to calm myself. I know my shock is temporary, but it remains with me, still. I tell my self I am not traumatized, the wounds on my feet are not as deep as the wounds of others.

(7)

It seems to have been an electrical problem that caused the fire on Ash Avenue. It has been a month, but the owner has sent no communication about the accident, about its possible permanent effects on the building's structure or safety. We tenants are no better. It crosses my mind: we have not even held some sort of meeting to brainstorm a strategy for repairs.

Yet we know the damage is significant—we are damaged. According to the firefighters, a handful of people were taken to the hospital for breathing smoke; a kid broke his arm jumping from the fourth floor; and my feet were burned going down the fire escape.

As for the building, the second and third floors are for the most part burned. Many of the apartment doors were forced open, electrical wires lay exposed in the sooty, black corridors, and everywhere the smell of smoke is overwhelming.

I meet my neighbor Lisa, a Puerto Rican woman, going down the stairs. She tells me the fire was due to an electrical problem inherent to the building. "My children," she said, "are traumatized. They're staying with their grandmother's until we can get out of here." She is looking for a new apartment. There are many people who want to leave the building.

Maybe she is being dramatic, but standing there with her in the blacken corridor, unable to lean casually against the wall without ruining my blouse, I decide I can no longer live on Ash Avenue.
My daughter decides to come to the rescue. We have always dreamed of living together in a brownstone in Brooklyn.

"We could have garden space at the rear and on the roof."

"We could have a pool for the kids, and we'd have family cookouts and fruit cocktails or iced tea."

"Who knows," she adds, "it might have decorative fireplaces and plenty of high windows to let in the sunlight"

And I say, "In the summertime, we'll go to concerts at Prospect Park, they'll have Tabou Combo playing *compas music*, or maybe Boukman Eksperyans, entertaining us at the sound of *rasin music*. Who knows?"

(8)

Two months have passed; it is now July. I'm in my new apartment. My daughter and I take great pleasure in decorating it. We found a large antique mirror with a carved wooden frame, which we placed above the sofa bed in the living room. We also bought some cheap shelves where we'll put books and a few trinkets. I hang my Manès

24

Descollines' painting, the Garibaldi, and the one my friend Ray painted after the fire, a collage my brother made, as well as a Georgia O'Keefe poster. I still have to buy frames for family photos.

The new building is in any case in better shape than the one on Ash Avenue. I tell myself I can invite friends and family over my home for dinner and they will not be afraid to take the elevator.

New York, 2005 & 2011

CHAPTER 3

THE DISAPPEARANCE OF MRS. GREENE

2005 AND 2011

How and why Mrs. Greene vanished from my life remains somewhat a mystery to me to this day.

When she became unavailable for me, I was totally confused about her reasons for leaving our relationship which, in my mind at least, was growing to become more than a casual encounter and a professional rapport. For, I longed for Mrs. Greene and myself to become friends so we could be there for each other to share our work, our lives, our joys and sorrows, our plans for the future and yes, our evocated pasts. I planned for leaving this solitary journey behind and begin a new life filled with productive and rewarding activities as well as leisure and pleasures; a classical concert at the local library, a jazz soirée at the Conservatory of Music, tea or coffee at a Korean or Chinese Café, a relaxing film at the movie theater, a walk on the beach or cooking couscous together, and yes, listening to some good Haitian or Brazilian music we like...

But Mrs. Greene had, for all this time, other plans, other projects she did not share and they did not involve me. Mrs. Greene had secrets; she was very private. While I was like an open book, she avoided self-disclosure.

It all started when I decided to volunteer at the neighborhood hospital; a major change in the monotony of my life. That morning, I put on my 2-piece professional suit, fixed my hair in a Haitian bun, put on some lipstick and headed for the local hospital's Research Department.

- I have an appointment with Dr. Kaplan.

It's the office on the left toward the end of the room, the secretary said, looking a bit perplexed and impressed.

Dr. Kaplan who interviewed me wanted to replicate a study on health issues among Korean immigrants. Since Flushing is home to a lot of Asian immigrants, including the Koreans, it's the ideal place to study and verify whether early medical intervention has an effect on the incidence of breast cancer among these immigrants.

What is your first impression of the study, he says, expecting a professional answer?

He is very respectful and straightforward. All he seems to care about is that I have the required degree and some experience in research.

I wrote my doctoral dissertation on the cognitive development of Haitian children, I told him, handing him a copy of my resume.

It seems to me self-evident that there should be less disease if a prevention procedure, like self breast examination for example or a mammogram is used. Dr. Kaplan gives me a copy of the paper to bring home to read and comment.

I am excited. There is a possibility that I may join a research team at the hospital. It will be interesting to participate in formulating hypotheses, collecting data and developing conclusions as well as ideas for future research. Asking questions about the world and explaining things have been preoccupations that go back to my childhood years and I have a Ph.D. in Psychology that is a testimony to my enduring interest, determination and ability for doing research.

I am dreaming already. I am a volunteer now but, perhaps, I may be hired and thus get a research position later…with a pay…I can come out of unemployment and become the professional I am supposed to be.

But Dr. Kaplan has something even better in mind: he is looking to put me in contact with Dr. F. of the Pediatric Department, who is doing a study in the field of child health which will be more related to my specialization in Child Development.

I, of course, am more interested in the child study given my background. The target population will be the kids who come to the free hospital clinic, most of them being immigrant children. I am hooked.

Dr. F. of the Pediatric Department who is originally from Argentina is engaged in a research effort to determine if the children who come to the Pediatric clinic are directly experiencing or witnessing violence in their community. This is a replicated study based on a prepared interview with the children. I must administer a questionnaire to children aged 8 to 16 and find out if they have experienced abuse or violence in their lives. My first question to them is:

"In your whole life, has anybody ever made fun of you, humiliated you or ridiculed you?"

Soon, I was able to administer and complete 54 interviews/questionnaires. She needed a total of one hundred for her statistical measures.

The respondents who are mainly the younger ones, aged 8 to 12, report they have been the victims of violence in their school environment. This violence takes many forms like being humiliated or turned into ridicule because one is different in one way or another. Or being chased after or even beaten by one's classmate. One can be turned into ridicule for being obese, wearing glasses or speaking another language…

Dr. F's study on child abuse and community violence has turned into a research on bullying. My findings don't show parents abusing children but children abusing other children within their school milieu primarily. It would seem according to the data I collect that differences are not accepted by the mainstream children and that the immigrant child feels it the most being the first to be rejected by bully peers.

One day, Dr. F announces she has good news for me. I am asked to formulate a research project that is better connected to my own interests:

"There is a Haitian child population at Jamaica Hospital in Queens and at Brookdale Hospital in Brooklyn", she says. "I will be more than happy to see you come up with ideas to develop understanding of their situation and how their problems can be solved."

She then introduced me to the resident doctor, Mrs. Greene, who is originally from Haiti, has studied to become a Doctor in Mexico and worked in California prior to coming to New York.

"It will be a good match", says Dr. F.

Mrs. Greene, the resident doctor and I have our first meeting at a Chinese bakery by my mother's building, not far from the hospital. We decided we want to interview the parents of children of Haitian descent about these children's immunization status. Moreover, we plan to examine the parents' cultural beliefs and practices related to illness and health.

Our rather simple and self-evident hypothesis is the children born here are better immunized than the children born in Haiti and therefore have less disease. We also anticipate that voodoo beliefs may influence cultural practices related to illness and health.

A month later, it's not so good news: there was a fire in my building and I get out by the fire escape burning my bare feet to the second degree. It took me two months to go back to the volunteer job at the hospital. Dr. F visited me and brought me flowers but there was no sign of Mrs. Greene.

That morning, when I entered the Pediatric Department on the fourth floor of the hospital's administration building, I said good morning but did not hear a response. It was rather a hardly audible "how are you?" from the secretary. Not a sound from the Department's head. I wondered what their problem is. Haven't I been working for a year in this place on a volunteer basis? What must be the cause of the hostility? The resident doctors all seem to have an attitude as if they were superior. They avoid eye-contact and don't greet you in the corridors. I have a doctorate for god's sake! One of my sisters is a medical doctor! I consider myself as worthy as you!

I have a better rapport with Dr. F. She has, over the course of time, let go of her initial skepticism and has learned to trust my abilities when she realized I am successful at getting this consent form signed by the parents. After all, it's a complicated and problematic study, a real Pandora box, where parents can be found to abuse their children. And that finding could have led to all sorts of consequences and legal troubles. Luckily, with my help, it was transformed into a bullying study...

There is no news from Mrs. Greene, the Haitian resident Doctor supposed to be a good match for me and with whom I am to conduct a study on Haitian children's immunization status. I speculate: may be she is giving me more time to recover from the fire and the burns. Will she, in the future, become my friend like I wish her to be? After all, my new building is not that bad and I can have people over. She doesn't have this passion for research like I do and seems content to provide medical care for the sick babies and children. Wasn't she supposed to be a good match? Why couldn't I have been a good match for Dr. F? What make two people match together? Is it their nation of origin or the color of their skin?

It's bad news. Mrs. Greene never calls me and has disappeared with our research project. I will never know whether it was carried through.

Bullies Are Everywhere

"Today we are faced with the pre-eminent fact that if civilization is to survive, we must cultivate the science of human relationships", said F.D.R. in 1945. But my experience at the local hospital shows that even among professionals, relationships are problematic and invisible boundaries are in place to prevent a situation of social harmony.

"Human beings are herd animals with a strong drive to bond. It's in our blood", wrote another, but the experience shows when race and ethnic differences are involved, barriers are erected to prevent interactions and feelings to normally develop.

Bullying may be a constant in the immigrant person's life. This form of bullying is not physical. It is silent, smart and is a form of racism used by adults to oppress other adults.

A study about the incidence of racism at the hospital would certainly reveal many accounts of rampant, racist practices to maintain the status quo and the minorities 'where they belong'.

As for Mrs. Greene and although she didn't share with me, she may have been a victim of this overall atmosphere herself. Who knows why she abandoned the research study and her relationship with me to go back to California where she came from?

Bonds of friendship are certainly difficult in a society where racism is prevalent and when they are confined within cultures, "good matches" are certainly hard to be found.

CHAPTER 4

HAITI WHY PLURALISM IS AN IMPERATIVE

2009

Chapter Four

Generally in the world today, these are times of positive change.

President Barack Obama was just awarded the Nobel Peace Prize for presenting, defending and executing an agenda of dialogue and harmony between peoples and nations. And, even though the return of the troops from Iraq has yet to be completed, and there is a complicated war in Afghanistan, and the Middle East conflict between Israel and the Palestinians is still not resolved, we are hopeful for a better, peaceful, world. The United States is also once again engaged in a close relation with its traditional allies in Europe, Asia, and multilateralism is seen again as the way to prevent and resolve the world's conflicts.

The cold war is really coming to an end: the United States is enjoying improved relations with China, Russia, South -East Asia... and North Korea has promised to return to the negotiating table and to stop its pursuit of nuclear armament which means that as Capitalism and Communism evolve, the fierce struggle between these two systems of government and ideologies is turning to a peaceful mode and is continuing through dialogue.

Iran remains a preoccupation: its determined pro-Palestinian and anti-Israel stand reinforces the fear of this country's nuclear-arm capacity-building. But Iran does not seem eager to be isolated and it is making an effort to maintain a dialogue with the rest of the world. Since a war between Israel and Iran is dangerous for not only regional peace but world peace, the concerned nations are keeping a watchful eye on the development of the situation and are proceeding on the negotiation path with care and caution.

As for the countries of Latin America, they are headed in a good direction: while populism continues to influence the politics of this region, representative democracy is a dominant trend. Credible elections are organized periodically in this part of the world although at times they are contested by the losing party. Furthermore, the leadership of these countries is determined to take charge of their economy and to develop alternative ideas and institutions that will facilitate economic development and favor better living conditions for all.

In Haiti, elections are coming again. President Préval is at the end of his second term in office, and many elective legislative and local spots are open. During his presidency, the president's main achievement was to build the national police, The Police Nationale d'Haïti. This agency works in conjunction with the United Nations contingent to improve security and as a result of their work, kidnappings have decreased. However, politically, conditions remain questionable as the last senatorial elections' results were not credible for many observers and very few people participated.

From an economic standpoint, everything remains to be done. There is a great need for basic services such as water, electricity and urban development; the country's infrastructure remains defective, there is no employment or investment Education and healthcare are also lagging behind.

These days the political debate is heating up on the occasion of the next legislative and presidential elections: the "Convention Nationale des Partis Politiques", a regrouping of eleven political parties, which had supported the president and his team at the beginning of his presidency, has formulated serious criticism of the government and is seeking unity among political, civic and other grassroots groups in order to present a viable alternative for the elections. For these militants whose personal agenda is and has been, in certain cases, since adolescence, combined with the quest for public good and the improvement of living conditions in Haiti, pluralism is important.

Of course, these parties have been on the political scene for quite a while. Their leadership, in their 50s, 60s and 70s, have put together political groups since the 1960s, as they were involved in the risky struggle against the Duvalier dictatorship. In many cases, they devoted their lives to the common good and they continue to struggle to bring about a pluralist democracy in Haiti that they intend to be part of. They are having a hard time achieving this ideal, but, just because they haven't succeeded and still persist doesn't make them merely ambitious job seekers – although they also need to become more representative, viable, and united and articulate programs and platforms that respond to the needs of the country and its people and the priorities of today's world.

The Meeting at the Croix-des-Bouquets Ranch

On this United Nations Day, the political actuality in Haiti is dominated by the reactions to the news of a meeting orchestrated by René Préval that gathered the representatives of the country's 570 communal sections in preparation for the forthcoming local, legislative and presidential elections.

I can only speculate about what this recent move of the president means and I see two different possibilities:

1) Préval intends to organize free and credible elections and he is giving his group the largest possible – nationwide – representation in order to win again the political power;

2) Préval is attempting to consolidate his personal authority through a single party with the largest possible basis.

I will have to wait for the situation to unfold in order to find out which interpretation best fits the conditions of our country.

One thing is certain: the president does not seem to be trusted by much of the population which fears a takeover by Préval and his allies. After all, the last elections organized by the Electoral Council under the presidency of Frantz Gérard Verret resulted in mostly Lespwa representatives being elected, and many think those elections were manipulated at least in some parts of the country. Besides, when the president himself was elected in 2006, he did not hesitate to have the crowds take the streets to enforce results that although favorable to him did not reach the required 50 percent plus one.

Another thing is certain: those Haitians who are not in the president's camp and are thus excluded from political participation will not accept this move to take over political power.

I anticipate difficult days ahead of us and those people that presaged a smooth transition from Préval II to the next government may have been deluding themselves.

In Haiti, It's Investment Time

Now that kidnappings have decreased, has our country become the land of opportunity for foreign investors? About five hundred of them visited and attended conferences in the capital, Port-au-Prince, during the month of October.

The tenth Forum of the Enterprises of the Caribbean just ended having facilitated experience-sharing and the signature of contracts where two hundred entrepreneurs from twenty countries participated. The conference lasted three days during which competitiveness, agro-business and tourism were discussed:

"Haiti is breathing a new air necessary to grow from its actual conditions to development", said the president of the forum while noting "the extraordinary agricultural potential" of our country.

A Forum on Commercial Promotion also took place to "discuss the questions concerning commercial promotion mechanisms as well as investment facilitation in the Caribbean."

The Haitian business sector welcomed the event noting that Haiti offers an environment conducive to business and that public/private partnership has become more than an empty word.

This whole business fever started with the HERO or Haiti Economic Recovery Opportunity Act of 2004. This act, signed by President Bush, offered a preferential treatment for Haiti for its apparel production providing the country develops a market economy and implements political pluralism and the rule of law.

Later, the U.S. Congress passed Hope II to facilitate job creation in the textile industry in Haiti.

Many businessmen are thus attracted by the prospect of producing and exporting at low cost which Haiti offers. This situation creates of course the opportunity for greater profit. In addition, the country presents opportunities in building infrastructure such as roads, ports, airports etc... as well as in tourism and agro-business ...

So, President Préval declared Haiti open to business and visitors have been coming to explore the possibilities. This is a move which takes place at the dawn of presidential and legislative elections to be organized in 2010.

I ask myself whether we have the social and political stability necessary to attract massive foreign investment in the country at this precise moment when nobody knows what kind of election we are going to have.

Why the big rush to elections?

In Haiti, there is a rush to organize elections while the debate continues on the question of single party-ism versus pluralism.

But why political parties to begin with, one may ask. Why can't we just go to elections and vote for someone who doesn't represent a political party? The answer is that while we might want more democracy than we have now, and want to improve what we have, we do not wish direct democracy which is characterized by the absence of political organizations that are ruled by democratic principles. We want to ensure that we are represented by persons who are members of organizations that abide to the rules and modalities of democracy. We want to give our political system a solid ground.

We want pluralism, meaning that we don't want to be ruled by a single party which wouldn't represent the wide variety of viewpoints and ideas out there; and thus wouldn't reflect the make-up and diversity of our society. Although we don't want too much diversity or too many parties, we recognize it's not always good for a people to be led by a single voice and clan.

Under a single-party situation, there is no debate or competition--all processes that are healthy for a balanced government. Furthermore, governing is marked by exclusion rather than inclusion. We want the largest-possible range of views and groups to be included – although they must find common ground among themselves through alliances, fusions and regroupings.

Besides, why would a single group want to grab it all? Doesn't that represent a violation of democracy itself, an encroachment of its very definition? Isn't that dictatorial rather than democratic? If we want to exclude some of the people who want to participate, what would be the basis and what would be the criteria for inclusion or exclusion? Isn't that a questionable, or even a potentially repressive and abusive practice?

These considerations, questions and apprehensions seem appropriate in the present conjuncture and should be a concern to all who wish a peaceful transition and stability in the country.

The rush to organize the legislative elections in Haiti can accomplish two things: first it would be a disadvantage for those who are not yet organized thus preparing a victory for those who are, namely those in power, the Préval camp; second, it would lay ground for a constitutional amendment in favor of the existing government so it can assure the permanence, and the "stability" sought to create a political environment for investment. So the argument goes...

Once again, there will be legislative and presidential competitions in Haiti, our sixth presidential election in twenty-three years (1987-2010) since our last constitution was adopted and massively approved by an enthusiastic electorate in March 1987.

Everyone was thrilled about the fact that "makout pa ladan l", true, but there was also the promise of democracy in our country. Since then, we have only witnessed an electoral process marked by mockery, fraud and deception; and even bloody repression. Obviously, not everybody felt positively excited that day!

According to the constitution we were so enthusiastic about, the Provisional Electoral Council was supposed to have been replaced by a permanent body whose characteristic is to be independent and whose duty is to organize competitions that are credible and impartial and thus accepted.

Political parties that were emerging at the time were supposed to have become better organized and be representative of broader sectors of the people while they present policies and programs that are responsive to people's needs.

But despite the expectations (and apprehensions) that were created at the meeting at Croix-des-Bouquets where Préval announced he was going to launch a large regrouping in the forthcoming elections, there is no reaction in the political community that matches these news and actions on the part of the president. While he seems successful at attracting many to his regrouping called "Inite" or Unity, the opposition remains characterized by divisions and dispersion as sixty-nine so-called political parties have registered to participate in the upcoming legislative elections.

Of course, some of these groups have put their forces together and formed some kind of "rasanbleman", but one doubts their ability to attract a large representation that could seriously compete with the other side since the votes will be generally scattered.

In other words, the Haitian people seem, if and when presidential elections take place, headed toward a similar situation as in 2006 where Préval was able to achieve a score of 48 percent and the second candidate scored only 11 percent. Will there be a second round this time?

In fact, Haiti, while confronting a period of transition from the repressive and dictatorial regime of the Duvaliers to an inclusive political system as proposed in the 1987 constitution, is the subject of a silent but intensely polarized debate.

This debate opposes anti-democratic forces to those who hold high the ideal and principles of a pluralistic government as our constitution wants and proposes it, based on the premises that our people want to participate and to improve the conditions of their lives.

The political events of 1985-86 indicated something new: this time the people took the streets not only to overthrow a government but to change a system that was repressive, dictatorial and retrograde. The people wanted a new system and those personalities who drafted the 1987 constitution were aware and understood this new element of our history. It wasn't as before a mere "transfer of power" as happened from Lescot to Estimé, or Estimé to Magloire, or Magloire to Duvalier. What was wanted was a transformation of the regime, a transition from exclusion to inclusion, from repression to freedom, from poverty to economic development.

This change has not yet happened in Haiti.

Caught between those who are not willing to bring about a functional democracy and those who are not yet able to do so, I ask myself when this new democratic system of government will see the light of day.

CHAPTER 5

INNER VIEW WITH KATYA D. ULYSSE OF "VOICES FROM HAITI"

Maryse Roumain: I studied at The Sorbonne, Columbia University, and the Graduate Center City University of New York—where I obtained a Doctorate in Developmental Psychology. I have a commitment to research and improving the lives of children.

I am the wife of a man who comes from a political family; he is endowed with strong political convictions. I am the mother of two wonderful children, and the grandmother of two amazing girls who are my joy and consolation. I have the responsibility to accompany all of them in solidarity on their journey on Earth. That is what I do.

I am blessed to come from a family that places education above all things. From an early age, I was attracted to philosophy, psychology, history, and politics. I am motivated and governed by a work ethic rooted in my family and in my people. I strongly value work.

I am a world music lover.

I have redefined myself many times and am at present an "unorthodox" writer of research, autobiographical texts, and political commentaries.

J'écris pour dire, j'écris pour me souvenir.

I have been involved as a community advocate and in political activities for a better world for a long time. I write about my life to tell and to testify that I am alive and that I contribute.

Voices from Haiti: What is your earliest memory?

Maryse Roumain: I remember being bullied and rescued from isolation by my best friend. We wrote each other letters. We had such a beautiful rapport. I lost my girlfriend to a "tonton macoute". He took her family away from our province to the capital city Port-au-Prince. I guess my friend had to betray me in order to "save" the ones closest to her. I suffered from abuse and was victimized by many. I have experienced friendship and its loss. I am deeply marked by and reminiscent of these encounters.

Voices from Haiti: What do you consider to be the most important event in your life?

Maryse Roumain: I wish it were the recognition of my contribution to make the world a better place. I wish it were the company and inspiration of God. I have His presence in my life—this goes back a long time.

Undeniably, it's been of utmost importance that I was able to reflect on my life and communicate to the public through my books: Life Goes On, a Reflective Diary (2009) and Evocations of My Past (2011). I published two political essays: Why Pluralism is an Alternative? (2010) and, Haiti: Vers Un Nouveau Départ (2011).

Writing and Publishing are for me new "raison d'être", a "raison de vivre." I have found my voice through this literary genre. I have found my occupation, in a sense. It's like a renaissance, a renewal of my potentialities.

Voices from Haiti: What is your greatest hope for Haiti in 2012?

Maryse Roumain: I hope the musician who is our president keeps being the dynamic person he has revealed himself to be. I hope, also, that we are able to democratize and modernize our economic and political system.

Voices from Haiti: What is your greatest fear?

Maryse Roumain: Anonymity

Voices from Haiti: If you could be anyone in Haitian history, who would that be and why?

Maryse Roumain: Haitian history being a history of men, I have trouble finding the woman I would like to have been. I'd like to have been a successful professional person who led a productive and meaningful life, but I don't know who that would be.

Voices from Haiti: What superpower would you like to have? How would you use it?

Maryse Roumain: I wish I had the power to influence life on Earth, politically, economically, socially, culturally and otherwise. Who knows? Perhaps, I could help God achieve his kingdom of equilibrium, peace, prosperity, and happiness for all.

Voices from Haiti: What is the main lesson you have learned in life so far?

Maryse Roumain: Not to be too trusting. Choose your companions carefully, though the prospect of a life without friends is a scary one.

Voices from Haiti: What words of wisdom do you live by?

Maryse Roumain: Enjoy my family life. Enjoy working. Live in peace with God. Cherish friendship. Care for my health. Respect Diversity.

CHAPTER 6

NOTES ON HAITI DEMOCRACY

A "democratic" government is one that is defined by a popular participation, a government "by the people and for the people."

Our Haitian constitution of 1987 presents and proposes a model of democratic government based on:

Periodic elections where representatives are elected, since they are the emanations of voters;

The organization of government in three components: the Executive, the Legislative and the Judiciary, that work separately and together to accomplish the tasks of the State;

The acceptance of civil liberties or rights and the acceptance of pluralistic participation.

Modern democracy has existed for some two hundred years in the countries of Western Europe and North America. This mode of government has traditionally been linked to societies that have reached a certain level of education and wealth. Democracy is mostly achieved at the cost of struggle against monarchy and dictatorship. It is, in many cases, the result of battles where the people and their leaders shed their blood.

In a democracy, tolerance is required for those individuals and groups who present political differences. These individuals and groups may, in effect, criticize and challenge those in power.

Change-over of political power is guaranteed by free and fair elections.

Generally, the countries that are passing from a dictatorship to a democracy go through a period conceived as a "transition". As its name suggests, this is an interim phase where the past is not yet completely erased and the future has not completely come to fruition.

Transition periods are not supposed to last forever. A country and its people are not to get locked in a transitional phase. This implies they are making their way to or heading toward a "final" stage which is not the transition itself but on that goes beyond or transcends it.

Democracy is an ideal that is never fully achieved. It supposes a struggle for its own development and maintenance and it can reverse to the former state of affairs. In a democratic government, the leaders and rulers of the transition may use methods of repression that are inherent to the former situation and so, civil liberties may be threatened. Besides, managing differences and opposition parties may sometimes be achieved with recourse to violence due to the residuals of a former dictatorship.

Democracy, however, represents a major improvement over other systems of governing. It offers superior means for resolving ideological and political conflicts and providing for the population's bien être.

Our country, Haiti, since the departure in 1986 of the Duvalier family has been undergoing a transition to democracy. This ideal goal however has been impossible to successfully conclude since the military and the "macoutes", the civil militia of the former regime, have led counteractions aimed at maintaining the old status quo.

Following the massive vote of the constitution in 1987, the Haitian people shed its blood in the context of elections that were violently interrupted by the "macoutes" and the military. Following this failure to take power through peaceful elections, Jean-Bertrand Aristide, the leader of the lavalas movement, was brought to power in 1990. But his government did not last. The military exiled him and his entourage 7 months after the December 1990 elections. He was, however, able to return to power in Haiti as he was accompanied by 20,000 marines under the democrat Bill Clinton's government. He proceeded to destroy the Haitian army's bases to replace them by a brand new police. But his government was far from a democracy. After Aristide 1, the government of his Prime Minister René Préval came to rule.

In Haiti today, there has been neither, free, fair, or credible election or alternance of political power according to democratic principles or even political parties or regroupings characterized by democratic structures, mass participation and well defined and specific programs and projects.

The current government of Michel Martelly seems unable to promote a democratic state of affairs.

These twenty-six years of transition have not yet led to a democratic government in Haiti. A representative democracy, as our constitution of 1987 defined it, is not in place As we want to periodically organize elections there is not real effort to achieve a free and fair voting process, and there is, every time, a deliberate attempt to put in place an Electoral Council which is dependent on the Executive branch of government so as to control the outcomes of the suffrage.

CHAPTER 7

NOTES ON CAPITALISM

Chapter Seven

Historically, Capitalism is presented as an economic and political system that succeeded feudalism, and brought about by the accumulation of capital or wealth in the hands of those individuals or groups of individuals (social classes) who aim to make a profit in this "mode of production and exchange", based on the exploitation of the working class.

Capitalism is based on the existence of the bourgeoisie (industrial, financial and commercial) and the proletariat or workers. Hence, the importance on the one hand of the private sector and on the other hand of the working class in capitalist formations.

Workers and the other exploited classes traditionally have struggled in order to replace the capitalist mode of production into a society where social justice would prevail and inequalities reduced, the ultimate goal being a "communist" society where all individuals would benefit based on their abilities and needs.

Capitalism is compatible with Imperialism where the latter is justified by the need to conquer new markets, for an expansion of the exploitative classes.

Capitalist societies represent a market economy ('économie de marché'), based on the laws of supply and demand that are related to competition and are independent of government measures.

Marxists, especially the Russian ruler Vladimir I. Lénine, described the capitalist countries of the early 20th century as having reached an imperialist phase, the "highest or supreme stage of Capitalism", characterized by military expansion, economic, political and cultural domination of third world, underdeveloped countries.

Marxist studies of the Haitian social formation describe it as semi-colonial and semi-feudal; semi-colonial, that is to say, officially independent while they are dominated by one or more capitalist, imperialist, countries. Semi-feudal, that is to say, essentially composed of poor landless peasants also called "2 halves" or in French "deux moitiés", who receive a portion of the harvest as payment for their services to landowners.

Today, we must take into account the masses of urban and rural unemployed and the middle class that has been expanding since the beginning of the 19th century. We must also take into consideration the phenomenon of migration that has affected all strata of Haitian society.

As for the bourgeoisie, it is composed of the commercial, the big landowners, the industrial and the finance sectors.

Communism became obsolete in Eastern Europe due to the failure of a planned economy ('économie planifiée') where the state dominated. But, in fact, chronic and recurring problems accompany the development of Capitalism as well, including the following:

Inflation or rising prices is a constant of capitalist society which is not balanced by a corresponding increase in wages;

Recession or high unemployment affect the working class and also the middle classes;

The inability to increase access to wealth and reduce inequalities, thus creating a larger gap between the rich and the poor and difficulty to have a larger middle class;

Stigmatization and criminalization of the poor;

Marginalization and segregation of those who are different.

Today, the capitalist world is shaken by an economic and social crisis characterized by the above problems and by austerity measures in response to the economic crisis; a situation that has resulted in contestation and social protests in several European countries.

In the United States, we are going through the largest real estate crisis in history where lenders have been unable to repay their debt to property owners and the banks that financed them. We are also seeing a rise in oil prices affecting all consumers.

This situation has resulted in government intervention in the economy in several capitalist countries.

CHAPTER 8

NOTES ON COMMUNISM

Communism is a sociological and political ideology, a set of ideas that were put forward by Karl Marx, F. Engels, Vladimir I. Lenine and Mao Tse Toung. It is based on an analysis of society into social classes and proposes that the exploited, particularly the working class or proletariat and the poor farmers (Mao) should organize into a political party, the communist party, and fight to conquer political power on behalf of the whole society, while building an egalitarian society through the reduction of social inequalities.

In communist countries, the State or Government, not the private sector, builds an economy that is designed to create as many jobs as possible. Education, health and housing are the government's responsibility. Sport and Physical Education are a priority. Arts and Culture are revolutionary in content, and national defense against enemies (both internal and external) is assured by a powerful military contingent.

Communism implies a universal and global vision and ideal. While it existed in Russia at first, it spread to countries of Eastern Europe, Asia and Latin America (Cuba).

Communism calls for the dictatorship of the proletariat and individual liberties give way to common interests.

Communism had to face different challenges: those militants known as Trotskists and Stalinists were the first to depart from an orthodox view. Then, the Maoists criticized the Soviet Union for revisionism leading to a split in the world communist movement. The fall of the Berlin Wall in the 80s led to the end of communism in Eastern Europe.

In China there has been gradually an abandonment of strict communist views and the adoption of market economy principles.

The People Republic of China is presently the second largest economy after the United States, presenting an astounding success on the economic front. As for Cuba, the last bastion of communism with North Korea, it continues to strive toward a market economy and an adjustment of political freedoms.

The first Haitian community party, the PCH, was founded in the years 1932-1934 within the context of the end of the US occupation of our country which took place in 1915-1934. Founded and led by high class intellectuals – Jacques Roumain, Etienne Charlier, Anthony Lespès – the party proceeded to an analysis of social, political and cultural issues and chose the motto *la couleur n'est rien, la classe est tout, in English skin color is irrelevant, social class is most important;* which dates back to the movement of the southern farmer Jean Jacques Acaau.

The party published its analysis in a booklet: Analyse Schématique 32-34 and fought for the instauration of democracy in Haiti against the post-US occupation regimes that sought to perpetuate themselves in power, against the prescripts of the constitution. The party's leaders, including internationally acclaimed writer, Jacques Roumain, experienced exile, prison, persecution and marginalization.

Within the context of the Second World War, the first Haitian communist party joined the anti-nazi group in the fight against Hitler's fascism and advocated for the establishment of an anti-fascist united front in Haiti. It is within this particular political context that it was agreed to join forces with president Elie Lescot who represented the dominant social classes' interests in Haiti. Jacques Roumain, one of the founders of the communist party, accepted to represent his country as ambassador to Mexico.

Jacques Roumain returned to Haiti in 1944. He had resigned his post as ambassador to Mexico in protest against Haiti's president Elie Lescot who wanted to remain in power contrary to the prescripts of the constitution. He was to die of disease and rather mysteriously soon after.

The leaders of the party including Etienne Charlier, Anthony Lespès, Michel Roumain and Max Sam continued the fight for a democratic Haiti were political pluralism would be allowed including the communists and the socialists.

These leaders founded the Popular Socialist Party in 1946 in the context of a broad movement aimed at overthrowing the Lescot government. The "revolutionary" movement of 1946 failed to bring about real change and the Parliament and the Military elected the black politician Dumarsais Estimé as president. The skin color issue – rather than the class issue upheld by the communists and socialists - had come to dominate the political debate. In 1957, François Duvalier, an ideologue of the skin color issue, founder of the journal Les Griots, was elected president under the Military's influence. He was to establish a dictatorship and a dynasty for thirty years. All dissent, but especially communists and socialists were severely crushed in these times where the United States and the Soviet Union struggled to dominate the world. Many dissenters and opponents to the Duvalier dictatorship were killed or jailed in the worst conditions; others were exiled.

This was a brief overview of the history of communism in Haiti where by now the left has come to accept democracy, as presented in our 1987 constitution, as the political alternative.

At present, we may speculate that Communism, as it was originally designed, has been exceeded and/or transformed both economically and politically. The benefits to society of a market economy, the initiative of the entrepreneurial class, the importance of the private sector for the development of a country's economy are no longer up for debate. Similarly, on the political end, ideological pluralism and the adoption of individual and public freedoms are the order of the day. We can say, however, that Communism, in its original concern and vision to eliminate inequalities and the "exploitation of man by man" remains an ideal. In today's world, we still dream of freedom, a goal of democracy and of equality, a goal of communism.

CHAPTER 9

NOTES ON SOCIAL DEMOCRACY, SOCIALISM

Socialism or Social-Democracy is a center-left ideology defined by an alliance of reformism and realism in economic and social matters. It is far removed from the revolutionary ideology of communism on the contrary seeking consensus among social actors.

Today, socialist or social democratic parties united under the umbrella of International Socialism represent a significant political force in democratic countries where they often come to share the political power.with rightists and center leftist groups.

Founded a hundred years ago, the International Socialist group is the worldwide organization of social democratic parties. It currently brings together 161 political parties and organizations from all continents that constitute a significant force in democracies around the world. Many of these parties are in power or are in various countries the main opposition force.

According to the literature, The Socialist International, whose Secretariat is located in London meets every three years. The world organization includes thematic and regional committees and has consultative status with the United Nations. It represents a set of principles including:

- Deepening Democracy in all aspects of life
- Promoting Cooperation among nations
- Defending human rights through the promotion of freedom, equality, security and prosperity

It defends ideas of peace, environmental protection and support to the development of Southern countries.

"Liberals and Conservatives have focused on individual liberty at the expense of social justice and solidarity while Communists have

claimed to achieve equality and solidarity at the expense of liberty."
As for the Socialists, they give equal consideration to the ideas of
Freedom, Social Justice and Solidarity.

The first haitian political party of that designation was the Popular
Socialist Party. In short PSP. The Party was founded in opposition to
the re-election of president Elie Lescot in 1946. After the former
Haitian Communist Party dissolved and,the death of its main
founder, Jacques Roumain, the former Communist leaders now
Socialist founded the Party leading the ideological struggle against
the followers of the skin color ideologues (Francois Duvalier), the
bourgeois liberals (Louis Dejoie), the populist Daniel Fignole) and
others.

The Socialists state as the Marxists that the social question is a
question of class, not of skin color. They favor the formation of broad
democratic alliances in which they militate against the dictatorship,
the Military and favor the advent of formal democracy in Haiti. They
have a newspaper "The Nation" in which they express their political
and ideological positions. Its members are subject to political
persecution by the governments of the time.

The psp was involved in the revolutionary movement in 1946 when
it defended the idea of the emergence of a regime respectful of civil
liberties and economic progress in the context of elections by the
parliament. It was close to the idea of the black landowner of the
south, Edgar Nere Numa. The Noiristes regrouped under the
leadership of Duvalier accuse them of belonging to the mulatto
nuance and take advantage of this situation to isolate.them.

The PSP is marginalized at the coming to power of Dumarsais Estime
and is dissolved by the military which bannish its newspaper, much
appreciated by the population, "The Nation". It cannot survive under
the noirist wave that swept over the country with François Duvalier,

the main ideologue of Noirisme, anti-communist and anti-socialist par excellence.

May 2012

CHAPTER 10

HAITI UPDATE (2012)

J'ai récemment écrit un texte sur mon pays, Haïti, qui présente certaines données politiques sur les cinquante dernières années (1957-2007) et une analyse de ces faits politiques. Ce texte qui doit bientôt être publié, je l'ai intitulé d'abord « Une Démocratie Dévoyée » pour rendre compte de la lutte incessante qui eut lieu, pendant cette période, entre les idées et les forces démocratiques d'un côté et celles dictatoriales (de François Duvalier à Jean-Claude Duvalier),. Dans cette lutte, les idées démocratiques ne purent résister face à l'assaut de la dictature qui se manifesta par la mise au second plan du Parlement, des partis politiques et des libertés publiques. De fait, cette lutte remonte à la fin de l'occupation américaine de notre pays en 1934 quand, une fois l'occupant parti, les classes politiques, auparavant mobilisées dans la lutte anti-américaine, se livrèrent sous l'influence marquée de « l'ancien » occupant, un combat acharné pour la prise du pouvoir et le bénéfice des ses privilèges économiques, sociaux et politiques.

Le titre « Démocratie Dévoyée » est pourtant loin d'être évident et accepté par tous pour caractériser cette période. Beaucoup sont en effet convaincus que l'avènement du prêtre de Saint Jean Bosco, Jean-Bertrand Aristide, à la présidence en 1990, marquait (enfin !) l'avènement de la démocratie chez nous. Ce que nous n'avions pu réussir quand Sténio Vincent avait voulu se faire réélire, ce que le fameux mouvement de 1946 n'avait pas accouché, ce que la lutte des démocrates contre le gouvernement de Magloire n'avait pu réaliser, nous l'aurions pu grace à la mobilisation des masses « lavalassiennes. ».

D'autres pensent que le retour de Jean-Bertrand Aristide encadré de 20,000 soldats américains en 1993 après qu'il eut été exilé 7 mois après son investiture, représentait un « retour à la démocratie ». Et comme par la suite, des élections (même frauduleuses) eurent lieu périodiquement, on en conclut qu'il existait en Haïti un régime de démocratie.

J'ai montré dans mes textes qu'il a existé sous Aristide et Préval un régime qui n'était pas basé sur le respect des institutions démocratiques, partis politiques, élections honnêtes, conseil électoral indépendant, etc. Caractérisé par l'autocratie (sous Aristide) et une espèce de laissez-faire apparente sous Préval, les libertés ne furent pas vraiment respectées. Bref, il s'agit plutôt, en Haïti, et toujours aujourd'hui, de transition vers la démocratie et cela fait vingt-six ans que cela dure.

S'agit-il d'une incapacité structurelle à réaliser la démocratie chez nous ou d'un manque de volonté politique ? Incapacité qui se manifeste non seulement au niveau des gouvernants, du gouvernement et de la gouvernance mais aussi des forces d'opposition qui elles, sont dispersées, incapables de s'unir même autour d'une plateforme électorale. Le Parlement, lieu par excellence de débats politiques donc d'un échange démocratique, ne fonctionne pas selon ces normes mais représente un espace où les jeux d'alliance sont plutôt personnels et répondent à des intérêts d'argent.

Maintenant que les gouvernements d'Aristide et de Préval font partie de notre passé politique, en quelque sorte, que faut-il penser du gouvernement Martélly qui lui a succédé ? Est-on aujourd'hui plus avancé sur l'agenda d'une démocratie représentative en Haïti ?

Le gouvernement de Martélly et de son groupe se caractérise par son empressement à developper des projets pour les plus démunis (accès à l'éducation pour tous, programme « aba grangou » etc.). L'une des marques du présent gouvernement est aussi son empressement à lier des relations avec ses voisins du Sud (et du Nord) et à engager la coopération de ceux-ci. Ce gouvernement insiste sur la nécessité de l'investissement étranger dans l'économie haïtienne, sur celle du développement du tourisme...

L'engagement de ce gouvernement du côté de la constitution ou de la démocratie n'est pas donné cependant. Il y a beaucoup de travail à faire pour en arriver là. Il est donc très difficile de lui trouver une étiquette. ...Il n'est pas évident qu'on ne revienne à la dictature et aux tendances autocratiques. Un trait du tempérament haïtien ? La lutte pour le pouvoir est, en Haïti, très exacerbée. Les classes politiques haïtiennes, pulvérisées au sein de dits partis politiques, se livrent un combat très dur pour le contrôle des privilèges de l'Etat.

L'exacerbation de nos luttes internes a donné lieu, une fois encore, à l'occupation de notre territoire national, sous la forme aujourd'hui des forces militaires onusiennes, sans pour autant que ces dernières puissent vraiment contrôler la situation et encourager des alternatives unitaires valables pour la nation. En Haïti, nous nageons dans la corruption et l'impunité et une dégradation des valeurs morales.

Quelques faits restent positifs : l'accueil favorable fait à la Constitution de 1987 qui propose d'établir dans notre pays une démocratie représentative et de favoriser la democratie (voir le vote massif de la Constitution). Et aussi, l'accueil favorable fait à l'organisation d'élections, à tous les niveaux, élections que la classe politique n'arrive pas à organiser comme elles doivent l'être mais qui attirent toujours une grande masse d'électeurs convaincus qu'ils ont un mot à dire sur leur sort politique, un « devoir civique » à accomplir.

Sur le plan économique, Haïti demeure l'un des pays les plus pauvres du monde. Le gouvernement Martélly a manifesté sa volonté de redressement sur le plan social d'une part en organisant des projets pour soulager la misère des masses ; d'autre part, en envisageant des d'améliorer la croissance et le développement économique par la

69

promotion de l'investissement étranger, l'établissement de « zones franches », le développement du tourisme..

Là aussi, il faudrait faire attention à ne pas mettre la charrue avant les bœufs, autrement dit à ne pas vouloir aller trop vite. Et les investisseurs étrangers l'ont bien compris, eux qui hésitent à aventurer l'engagement de leurs capitaux alors que le pays n'est ni stable politiquement ni prêt sur le plan des infrastructures et de l'organisation politique.

Avril 2012.

Chapter 11

Preserving our Oral Literature (2013)

In 2009, I presented some 12 Haitian folktales targeting storytellers and the children's audience that listens and interacts with them, to be published in an anthology.

These folktales were part of Mimi Barthelemy's collection, a writer, storyteller and actress based in Paris who has done extensive research and performing to present them to a broad audience – mostly French but not exclusively – eager to be entertained and participate in the Haitian cultural experience and imaginary world.

As for myself, I had translated in English with minor adaptations for a youngest audience of children primarily from the New York community.

Today, I want to publish those folktales individually. After all, while some anthologies are available, our children do not have the advantage to benefit from a tradition which was alive and precious – but today lost – when we were kids ourselves. And we sat either on chairs or on the floor around our favorite storytellers, our servants who came from the countryside and the remote mountains, in a room lighted by a kerosene lamp where the obscurity surrounding us was an accomplice to the creation of a surreal and magical and sometimes fearful atmosphere these folktales often convey. Hence, the creation of the *krab nan kalalou children's book collection*.

Haitian literature – including children's literature – is currently expanding due to an incredible and somewhat mysterious surge in creativity during this prolonged period of transition to democracy and literacy. Many among us are engaged in the practice of literary creation and some of us have produced works that are appreciated by local readers and have as well received international attention and appreciation.

And, while this is happening, I want to turn to our folktales and re-create them in a new format – that of the book – to transmit this important aspect of our cultural heritage which reflects in such imaginative and artful ways our identities (see the tales of Bouki and Malis which portray the Stupid and the Trickster), our epic battles against enormous monsters (see Ti Fou and the Monster of Darkness), our magical inclinations and views of world phenomena (see Tezen and Sefi and the Magic Orange Tree), our denunciation of those in power (see horse, frog and the princess as well as frog and the key to the water), etc.

First, I want to acknowledge the Haitian people for creating and preserving its oral cultural heritage which has survived slavery, colonial domination and the predominance of Western cultures in our lives. Although our storytelling tradition seems to loose ground, even in Haiti, we are thankful that the tales have been preserved in various formats, languages and versions. I also want to acknowledge the storytellers and the various cultural programs and institutions that make use of our folktales.

I want to acknowledge that before our written literature, which goes back to the 19th century, there was our oral folk-literature transmitted from generation to generation by word of mouth and the origins of which we have no way of knowing. It existed before writing began carried on by those actually unlettered but who nevertheless were fond of works of imagination. It survives through storytelling and initiatives such as this one which carries it to the written level.

CHAPTER *12*

Past, Present And Future: The Fostering Of Our
Identities (2013)

Is who we are – as a people, as a person - a reflection of who we were as a people, as a nation? Are we the product of our national history or at least influenced by it? Isn't it an absolute necessity to infuse in our young the knowledge of their past in order to develop a sense of civics, a feeling they are determined, defined, characterized – at least in some ways - by our founding fathers' and mothers' history; in order to make them strong enough to confront the difficulties of the present, the destruction, degrading and devaluation of their self-image and self-esteem?

While for a long time the teaching of history in schools has been linked to the conception that it is about fostering a sense of national identity and civics, it is much clear today that a sense of identity, either personal or national, is something one forges for oneself and is fashioned from many sources.

Let's make no mistake about it: our national history is an essential aspect of our own identity – although not enough to sustain its development. And, according to well-known sources "all human beings need their past" to understand their society and how it changes, but the story of our past needs also to be religious, social, economic, literary, musical and artistic, etc. all this influencing the multiple facets of our identities.

Let's face it. As a people and as nationals of the Nation of Haiti, our identities, in various parts of the world, have been constantly challenged. From Cuba's sugar cane plantations in the 19th century when we were called *haitiano maldito, negro de mierda* to the New York of the 1980s when we were considered the carrier of AIDS and to today when our independence and sense of pride is mocked by the presence of UN troops on our soil. And while being challenged, we learn to keep our heads high, to draw and derive emotional strength and courage from who we are which is based on who we were and the identifications we have made along the way with those among us who carried the struggle – Martin Luther King, Malcom X, Nelson Mandela, Jacques Roumain and Jacques Stephen Alexis – inside and outside, further, those who continued the fight.

The primary lesson we draw from our past is that we're a people struggling to maintain our self and culture. While our leaders led epic battles against the powerful of this earth, they have lost many. Let's mention from Columbian times, the Taino Queen Anacaona whose struggle to maintain Ayiti's independence and culture was crushed and her people slaughtered, what is known in history as the 'Alcantara Massacre' where no one was spared by the Spanish conquistadores. Let's also mention Toussaint Louverture who gave the Haitian freedom from slavery as well as autonomy from France who was imprisoned in Fort de Joux, a dungeon in the Jura Mountains in France, where he died. And, Jean-Jacques Dessalines who carried on the struggle was assassinated while the country remained divided between the blacks and the mulattoes. As for Henri Christophe, the builder of palaces and citadels, he also died of unnatural death when his closest allies abandoned him and he was accused of using forced labor against his people and of distributing land and favors to his kingdom's elite. His rival in the South, Alexandre Pétion, had to abandon his dream of a democracy for Haiti, when the Senate wanted to impose his rule. And, since then, we have been struggling for a democratic government in Haiti.

Our history is a history of struggle and the main lesson we can draw from it is that we are a people who has and must continue to fight...for our independence, our cultural integrity, our economic survival and our political rights.

Yes, we are the descendants. We share the blood. We share a common past and because of that we are who we are. In our eyes as in those of others, those foreigners who look at us as those who are "always making history", despite being repeatedly crushed, like Anacaona, Toussaint Louverture, Jean-Jacques Dessalines, Henri Christophe, Alexandre Pétion and the others.

CHAPTER 13

POEMS

Why Diversity?

Diversity is inclusive not exclusive

Diversity reflects the way things and people are in the real world

Diversity implies the acceptance of those who disagree

Diversity signifies a non Manichean view of the world

Diversity implies the respect for differences

Accepting diversity means an attitude of tolerance

Diversity means non-sectarian, non-fanatic and the search

for harmony and peace

The respect for diversity is not synonymous with the abandonment of one's own principles, beliefs and opinions

The respect for diversity does not signify a perpetual need for consensus but acknowledges the desire for continued interlocution and dialogue

The respect for diversity does not mean all ideas are equal

Diversity is synonymous with the search for balance and equilibrium: it is the opposite of extremism and caricature.

O Femme

Le temps d'un regard

Et un lien s'est créé

Une reconnaissance réciproque

Une appréciation mutuelle

- Mystères-

Je raconte des histoires d'amitiés perdues

Femme sensuelle

Femme lesbienne

J'enregistre et me souviens.

Femme Créatrice

Ton image et mon écriture s'interpellent, s'accordent

Et s'entrelacent

-Magie du Talent -

- Miracle du Verbe -

Tu dessines les formes du récit qui prend corps

En noir et blanc

Et de tes tableaux se dégage la vérité de mes mots.

Maryse Noël Roumain

(Poème rédigé à l'occasion de ma collaboration avec la dessinatrice Beatriz Olliveti).

Où sont passés les enfants de Bagdad?

La guerre en Irak commencée le 20 mars 2003 n'a pas encore
pris fin aujourd'hui que je suis dans mon nouvel appartement

Je suis de ceux et de celles qui croyaient sa justification

Cousue de fil blanc.

La ville est bombardée, la ville est détruite

Que sont devenus ses habitants ?

Où sont passées les armes de destruction massive

The weapons of mass destruction are nowhere to be found

Saddam, the dictator, is nowhere to be found.

Où sont les laboratoires mobiles de recherche biologique
annoncés ?

Et les usines d'armes chimiques et les bunkers ?

La justification est cousue de fil blanc :

« C'est de la merde ! Rien ne se tient ! » aurait lancé quelqu'un à l'ONU

Des conquérants se lancent dans le combat sans l'aval

Du Conseil de Sécurité des Nations-Unies

Une opération qui devait en principe durer trois mois

Est encore en cours aujourd'hui.

Où sont passés les enfants de Bagdad ?

« Opération accomplie », annonce le président des Etats-Unis. Où est donc l'échec annoncé ?

Où est passé Saddam ?

Finalement sorti de son trou, les yeux hagards, la barbe longue et les cheveux ébouriffés.

Saddam est jugé

Saddam est mis à mort

Mais la conquête de l'Irak n'aura pas lieu.

Author's Biography

(February 2015)

Born in southern Haiti, in the province of Les Cayes, Maryse Noël Roumain immigrated to the United States at the age of 19. She studied Psychology at the Sorbonne in Paris, Teachers College-Columbia University and the Graduate Center-City University of New York where she obtained a Doctorate in Developmental Psychology.

She worked for the New York City Board of Education and the New York State Education Department and subsequently, in Haiti, for education projects sponsored by the United States Agency for International Development and the Inter-American Development Bank. Maryse Noël Roumain also worked at the Ministry of Education in Port-au-Prince as a Counselor to the Pre-school Department.

She has been working for a better Haiti from the age of 20, in Paris, New York and Haiti. Maryse is now deeply involved in transformational politics to make the world a better place. She became a non-fiction writer to reach out to people all over. She published books and holds a blog at www.maryseroumain7.wordpress.com. She is also on Facebook.